INTRODUCTION

To observe the beauties of nature, few places in the world are as satisfying as New Zealand and, in particular, the Southern Lakes region of the South Island.

It is perhaps the fault of the Western World that colonisation has ruined the true splendour of nature as it always has been, but in the southern areas of New Zealand much of the land is still as it was intended to be.

The urban cities of the South Island of New Zealand are mainly situated on the east coast, but as one travels further west, an abundant wonderland opens up before visitors.

Access is only difficult into the remote region of Fiordland. Before reaching there, visitors can easily travel through the beautiful area of the Southern Lakes. Fed by streams, the rivers flowing from the snow covered island's backbone, the Southern Alps, the Southern Lakes are high on the agenda of any tourist coming to New Zealand. The diversity of mountains and plains that surround them adds to the attraction of lakes such as Tekapo, Wanaka, Hawea, Wakatipu, Te Anau and Manapouri. Europeans reached this land in the middle of the last century, mainly in search of gold, but today a booming tourism industry has opened this beautiful region for all to become enriched by its splendour.

LAKE TEKAPO & LAKE ALEXANDRINA

The deep south of New Zealand was largely inhabited by immigrants from Scotland during the late 1800's. They must have marvelled at the similarity in the lake region of the interior, to their homeland.

The early musterers relied heavily on their sheepdogs on the large sheep stations ***(top left)*** while scenes like the Church of the Good Shepherd, reaching into the surrounds of Lake Tekapo ***(above)***, could have been taken straight from a picture book of the Scottish Lochs.

One of the smaller lakes of the central South Island is Lake Alexandrina, at its most beautiful at dusk ***(top right and opposite page)***.

MT COOK

Among the grandeur of the towering mountains of the Southern Alps, lie many spectacular and secluded valleys, such as the Hooker Valley ***(left)***.

The diversity within the natural splendour of the region is shown in the many glaciers which flow slowly westward from the peaks towards the coast, such as the Tasman Glacier ***(above)***.

At ground level, Mount Cook Lillies are abundant in places like the Hooker Valley in South Canterbury, while, always in the background, Mount Cook (Aoraki) 3764 metres towers above the valleys and Lake Pukaki ***(right)***.

LINDIS PASS & LAKE OHAU

Heading south, the early pioneers found a way through the rolling, mountain terrain via the Lindis Pass into Central Otago ***(top and bottom left)***, with the Scottish influence again being brought to the fore in old stone farm buildings ***(left centre)***.

The high country of the South Island contains most of New Zealand's largest sheep stations, such as Lake Ohau Station ***(above)***. Compared with the more fertile areas of the coastal south, these stations carry far less stock numbers per hectare, with sheep and cattle grazing casually in their foothill surroundings.

These areas are sparsely populated and driving through areas like the MacKenzie Country, visitors will sense the freedom of the open countryside.

LAKE HAWEA & LAKE DUNSTAN

The Lindis Pass opens a whole new region – and one of New Zealand's most beautiful – as Central Otago welcomes visitors to the Southern Lakes. The first is Lake Hawea ***(above left)*** with the Sentinel and Terrace Peaks as its backdrop. Most of the Southern Lakes are among the largest in New Zealand but some of the smallest, like Lake Dunstan ***(top right)*** offer tourists and outdoor sportsmen chances to tramp, swim and fish in total freedom.

Rivers, such as the Upper Clutha ***(above)*** are perfect for the fly fishermen.

The seasonal changes from winter ***(above right)*** and summer ***(below)*** gives places such as Lake Hawea an ever changing face.

LAKE WANAKA

A popular holiday spot for many New Zealanders is tree-lined Lake Wanaka, ***(left)*** on the outskirts of Mt Aspiring National Park. The resort township of Wanaka hosts summer holiday makers who enjoy fishing, boating and water skiing, tramping and a simple, relaxed way of life. In winter, skiing is the main attraction on the surrounding skifields.

Mt Aspiring ***(top)*** is one of the most spectacular peaks of the Southern Alps and, because of its shape, is known as the "Matterhorn of New Zealand". At 3027 metres, it is also one of the highest peaks in the region. The tranquillity of Glendhu Bay ***(above)*** makes it a favourite spot for campers and water skiers.

INVERCARGILL
OAMARU
MT. COOK

CROMWELL & ALEXANDRA

On the Kawarau River in the Cromwell Gorge is a small power station, The Roaring Meg ***(top left)***, supposedly named after a raucous, red-headed barmaid of the gold mining days. A centrepiece of the town of Alexandra – the community hub of Central Otago – is the Alexandra Bridge ***(top right)*** across the Clutha River. One of the most controversial hydro power projects in New Zealand was the Clyde Dam which created the man-made Lake Dunstan and wiped out much of the historical mining town of Cromwell. The confluence of the Kawarau and Clutha Rivers ***(above)*** was flooded to form Lake Dunstan in the 1980's and much of Cromwell was rebuilt to house the project workers.

The Kawarau River flows through the Cromwell and Kawarau Gorges, linking Lake Wakatipu and Lake Dunstan.

QUEENSTOWN & LAKE WAKATIPU

One of the most spectacular scenic sights in New Zealand is from the Skyline gondolas ***(left)*** which rise 446 metres above the resort town of Queenstown.

Marvellous views of Lake Wakatipu and the imposing, snowclad Remarkables mountain range attract tourists from all around the world.

QUEENSTOWNS
Chico's
BAR & GRILL
HERCRAFT
LERS MILL
CAMBIO

QUEENSTOWN

Jutting out of the Frankton Arm of Lake Wakatipu is Kelvin Heights ***(top right)***, the site of one of New Zealand's most spectacular golf courses.

The Queenstown waterfront ***(bottom right)*** has changed its face since the days of the last century, when many of the needs of goldminers in the surrounding areas were shipped up Lake Wakatipu from Kingston. Today, modern hotels surround Queenstown Bay, with only the historic hotels surround Queenstown Bay, with only the historic Eichardts Tavern remaining from the vibrant gold mining era.

ADVENTURE ACTIVITES

Because of its many and varied outdoor activities, Queenstown has been dubbed the Adventure Capital of the World. Bungy jumping ***(top left)*** originated in its commercial form near Queenstown at the historic Kawarau Bridge while, in the winter season, skiing at Coronet Peak or the Remarkables ***(top right)*** brings thousands of visitors to the region.

The Edith Cavell Bridge ***(bottom left)*** spans the Shotover Canyon, through which the Shotover Jet boats have thrilled more than a million adventure seekers. A relatively new adventure is parapenting and tourists marvel at their scenic surroundings on their tandem rides with professional parapenters.

For the more sedate water lovers, there's a ride across Lake Wakatipu to Walter Peak on the historic steamer, the T.S.S. Earnslaw ***(top)*** - a far cry from the rough and tumble of white water rafting ***(above)*** on the Shotover and Kawarau rivers.

ARROWTOWN

Just 20 kilometres from Queenstown is the quaint gold mining town, Arrowtown. One of its many historic buildings is St John's Church, ***(top left)*** built in 1873. The Lakes district Museum ***(top right)*** is framed by an avenue of magnificent sycamore trees, a feature of Arrowtown, while the surrounding countryside is also a blaze of colour - thanks to the variety of trees that cover the landscape ***(above)***.

Kept as they were built more than a century ago, miners' cottages ***(right)*** take visitors to Arrowtown back in time to the days when millions of dollars worth of gold was panned out of the Arrow River during the rush of the 1860's.

ARROWTOWN BOROUGH COUNCIL

LAKE HAYES

There is probably no more serene or lovely sight in the whole of New Zealand than Lake Hayes ***(left)*** on a calm day with autumn colours completing the beauty.

Named after one of Central Otago's most colourful pioneers, Bully Hayes, Lake Hayes attracts photographers pioneers from all over the world, eager to capture its beauty. To keep its tranquil image, no powered boats are allowed on the lake, which nestles under the Remarkables and Coronet Peak.

Smaller than the other main Southern Lakes - Hawea, Wanaka, Wakatipu and Te Anau - Lake Hayes hasn't attracted a town on its banks, with only a few private homes dotted along one shoreline.

SHOTOVER RIVER & SKIPPERS

When the gold rush of the 1860's hit Central Otago, it was said that, in Skippers Canyon ***(top, above left and opposite)***, the Shotover River contained almost an ounce of gold in every square foot of the river bed. But the extreme hardships of Skippers, especially in the bitter winter months, made gold very hard to extract and there is still reputed to be a harvest of the valuable metal in the river. Today there is bungy jumping from the spectacular Skippers Bridge, over 100 metres above the Shotover River - itself a gold mine for modern day adventure operators. The infamous Skippers Road is only for the best and bravest of drivers but visitors can still travel as the old pioneers did on horseback along the Moonlight Trail ***(above right)***.

As the Shotover River winds its way out of the steep walls of the Skippers Canyon, it opens up to gravel beaches as it heads towards Lake Wakatipu at Arthurs Point ***(above)***.

But everywhere you venture in this beautiful Wakatipu Basin, new bounteous views extend before you. The Kawarau River ***(opposite, top left)*** has The Remarkables mountain range as a backdrop, and the hillsides in any direction contain a host of wonderful colours and scenic delights. For trampers, the region is a tranquil wonderland, full of surprises.

With New Zealand being a very young country by international standards of colonisation, Central Otago's gold mining history makes it one of the few areas in the country featuring rustic old buildings of days gone by ***(right)***.

HISTORIC OTAGO

Throughout this lower portion of the South Island's interior, there are remnants of the past. History is full of stories of hardened pioneering families, able to accept and then beat off the brutal coldness of snow covered winters, to eke out a living. After the gold rush days, those who chose to stay turned to agriculture and, today, to tourism.

The old buildings of Central, Otago are usually made of the local Central Otago schist stone, such as the jailhouse at Styx ***(top left)***. The reality of living in these stone cottages through the ravages of winter is graphically shown ***(centre left)***, while old stone ruins of buildings which have not survived the rigours of time, are dotted everywhere south of the Lindis Pass ***(bottom left)***.

The Scottish heritage of many of the early farmers in Central Otago is shown in the stone architecture, such as this two-storeyed barn near Arrowtown ***(above)***.

LAKE WAKATIPU & GLENORCHY

At the head of Lake Wakatipu lies the remote township of Glenorchy which, until relatively recently, was only accessible by boat steamer. But, in the early 1960's the construction of the Glenorchy Road opened the area, with trampers and climbers being able to drive to the world famous Routeburn and Greenstone tracks leading into Fiordland.

The road winds past Mt Creighton Station ***(above)*** and offers views of other high country sheep stations such as Mt Nicholas ***(top left)***.

Past Glenorchy, travellers can now travel by jetboat excursions along the Dart and Ress rivers ***(top right)*** at the head of Lake Wakatipu and finally arrive at the aptly named destination at the foot of the Southern Alps, "Paradise."